Funny Pet Poems

Hatty Jones

Published by Hatty Jones, 2025.

While every precaution has been taken in the preparation of this book, the publisher assumes no responsibility for errors or omissions, or for damages resulting from the use of the information contained herein.

FUNNY PET POEMS

First edition. February 10, 2025.

Copyright © 2025 Hatty Jones.

ISBN: 979-8230834908

Written by Hatty Jones.

Funny Pet Poems

Welcome, animal lovers, pet parents, and poetry enthusiasts! If you've ever lived with a pet, you already know—they're cute, they're cuddly, and they're absolutely hilarious! From dogs who refuse to fetch, to cats who believe they rule the universe, to birds with a questionable vocabulary, our furry, feathery, and even scaly friends never fail to entertain us.

This book is a playful celebration of the weird and wonderful world of pets, told through the magic of poetry. Inside these pages, you'll find mischievous hamsters, sneaky snack-stealing dogs, fish with big dreams, and cats who take their job of knocking things over very seriously. Each poem is a little tribute to the funny, messy, and love-filled chaos that comes with sharing our homes (and our hearts) with animals.

So whether you're a proud pet owner or just someone who enjoys a good laugh, get ready for a collection of rhymes that will make you giggle, nod in agreement, and maybe even shake your head at how accurate these pet antics really are.

Now, sit back, relax, and let the pet poetry begin! Just be careful—your cat might knock this book off the table before you finish reading.

Dogs & Their Shenanigans

The Midnight Mission

By moonlight's glow, he sneaks around,
A sock-thief king, so sly and sound.
With silent steps, he stalks his prize,
A fluffy sock in his eager eyes.
One quick snatch, then off he darts,
Leaving chaos in human hearts.
Behind the couch, beneath the chair,
A sock graveyard hidden there.
No ransom note, no grand reveal,
Just missing socks—a mystery real.

The Sock Sniffer's Secret

He sniffs them out both near and far,
From laundry piles to dresser drawers ajar.
No sock is safe, not one will last,
They vanish quickly, stolen fast.
Striped or plain, thick or thin,
He loves them all—let the games begin!
A single sock, a pair undone,
His mission's clear, his crime is fun.
You search in vain, you shake your head,
But he's curled up, sock in bed.

One Sock at a Time

You start the day with matching feet,
By noon, one's gone—another defeat.
Where do they go? You may not know,
But check the yard, beneath the throw.
A sneaky grin, a wagging tail,
This furry thief will never fail.
You chase, you plead, but it's no use,
Your socks are his, there's no excuse.
So buy more pairs, but don't forget—
One sock's a prize, the game's not set!

Laundry Basket Loot

The laundry basket stands so tall,
A tempting sight—he wants it all.
He dives right in, a daring pro,
Emerging with a sock in tow.
You holler, chase, but he runs fast,
Your favorite pair—he's made it past!
Through the house, a joyful sprint,
The sock now wears his drool imprint.
He flops down proud, a champion bold,
With his stolen prize, so soft to hold.

The Sock Bandit's Hideout

Where do they go? Oh, who can say?
They vanish fast, just slip away.
Under the bed? Behind the chair?
In corners dark? They're everywhere!
A secret stash, a hidden trove,
Inside his crate, deep in the cove.
You find them later, chewed and worn,
Your favorite pair—now ripped and torn.
But in his eyes, he's done no wrong,
A sock's a toy, and fun lasts long.

The Foot Smell Fanatic

The smellier, the better—his preference is clear,
A sock worn all day is his souvenir.
Fresh ones are fine, but they lack that zest,
The ones on your feet? Those are the best!
You kick them off, stretch and yawn,
Turn for a second—poof, they're gone!
Under the couch or behind the door,
Your dog is victorious once more.
No shame, no guilt, just pure delight,
Another sock thief's perfect night.

The Chase is On

You spot the thief, sock in his jaws,
His tail wags fast—he loves your pause.
You lunge, he leaps, a game is set,
A tug-of-war with no regret.
He dodges left, then dashes right,
His grip is firm, his hold is tight.
Through the hall and out the door,
Your sock is gone—forevermore.
You sigh, you groan, you let him win,
Tomorrow's game will start again.

Sock Wars: The Family Feud

It starts off small—a single pair,
Then suddenly, socks disappear everywhere.
Mom's are gone, Dad's are too,
Little brother's sock? Nowhere in view!
The family scrambles, searches wide,
But the culprit's tail wags in pride.
His stash is found—twenty deep!
A sock-hoard pile, a dog's prized keep.
One by one, they're saved at last,
Until the next sock heist is cast.

Sock or Toy? The Age-Old Debate

A sock's not food, a sock's no bone,
Yet somehow, he makes it his own.
He shakes it, tugs it, throws it high,
His treasured toy, his reason why.
You buy him plushies, ropes, and chews,
Yet still, your socks are what he'll choose.
Soft, just right, perfect to grip,
Better than any toy from a trip.
So you give up, accept defeat,
And hide your socks—until next week.

The Sock King's Throne

Upon the couch, he takes his seat,
A sock beneath his little feet.
With head held high, he rules with pride,
A loyal thief, no need to hide.
His kingdom vast, his treasures grand,
A stolen sock in every hand.
His people search, they beg, they plead,
But he just wags—he has no need.
For in his mind, he's won the prize,
The Sock King reigns with laughing eyes.

The Day He Retires

One day, the socks will all be safe,
No more thefts, no midnight chafe.
The laundry will sit undisturbed,
No sneaky paws, no stolen curb.
A quiet house, no frantic chase,
No missing pairs, no hiding place.
But on that day, something's amiss—
The house will lack that sock thief's bliss.
For though he's naughty, wild, and bold,
His sock heists are worth more than gold.

The Slobber King

His jowls are big, his tongue is wide,
A tidal wave he can't keep inside.
One shake of his head and there it goes,
A stream of slobber from his nose.
It lands on walls, it drips on floors,
It clings to chairs, it coats the doors.
His water bowl? A splashy mess,
His love for drool? You'd never guess!
You wipe it up, but what's the use?
A fresh supply is always loose.
He wags his tail, so proud, so cool—
In his world, the drool rules!

The Waterfall Waltz

The moment he drinks, the dance begins,
A wobbly waltz, the mess sets in.
His mouth can't hold what he just drank,
So down his jowls, it forms a plank.
A waterfall spills from his sloppy grin,
Dripping, splashing—where to begin?
Paws are wet, the floor's a lake,
A slip, a slide, a big mistake!
Yet look at him, without a care,
His drooly face, his happy stare.
He lives by one unshaken rule—
If it's wet and messy, then drool rules!

The Wettest Welcome

You step through the door, he comes in fast,
A big, wet kiss—a full-time blast!
His tongue is out, his slobber flies,
A damp surprise between your eyes.
Your shirt's now soaked, your hands feel slick,
Your face is sticky, your arms won't quick.
You laugh, you groan, you wipe it clean,
But another round's already seen.
He doesn't know, he doesn't care,
That drool is dripping everywhere!
No handshake, hugs, or subtle cues—
He greets the world with drool rules!

The Dinner Disaster

Mealtime starts, his eyes are locked,
A puddle forms, the floor is rocked.
His lips start quivering, drip by drip,
A flood arrives—oh, watch your grip!
You give him food, he takes a bite,
The mess he leaves? A frightful sight!
His bowl's a swamp, his chin is wet,
Your patience tested—place your bet!
Will he stay dry? Not a chance,
His drool will do its slimy dance.
For every meal, there are no tools,
Just proof that here, drool rules!

Drool Trails & Slippery Tales

You spot the path, the slimy clue,
A trail of drool both fresh and new.
Across the tiles, around the chair,
A shining streak, beyond repair.
You wipe it once, you wipe again,
Yet somehow, still—it's back, my friend!
One shake of his head, one sloppy grin,
And there it is—he strikes again!
Like an artist with his brush,
He paints in slobber, smooth and lush.
No cleaner strong, no mop or tools,
Can stop the fact that drool rules!

The Couch is No Longer Yours

The couch was yours—at least before,
Now drool has claimed it evermore.
A dampened patch, a sticky seat,
A puddle growing by your feet.
His chin rests down, his eyes half-closed,
A peaceful sight—you stay composed.
But then he dreams, he gives a snore,
And suddenly—here comes the pour!
The cushions soaked, the smell is strong,
You sigh and know this won't be long.
The couch is his, there are no fools,
In this domain, drool rules!

The Car Ride Crisis

He hops inside, he takes his place,
A goofy grin across his face.
Excitement grows, he starts to pant,
A flood begins—you don't recant.
Drool on windows, drool on seats,
A slime tsunami on the sheets.
His jowls are loose, his lips let go,
The car is now a drool show!
You grab a towel, you brace for more,
The ride's begun—a soaking tour.
By the time you reach your chosen pools,
It's clear to see—drool rules!

The Vet Visit Slime Show

The vet calls in, it's time to go,
He wags his tail—he doesn't know.
Excitement builds, the drool begins,
His tongue flops out—it never ends.
By the time he's in, the place is slick,
The floor's a mess, the walls are thick.
The vet just laughs, the nurse just grins,
They've seen this show—it soon begins.
A gentle shake, a mighty spray,
Drool flies off in full display.
They clean, they sigh, they grab more tools,
For in this room, drool rules!

Beware the Drool Whip!

You think you're safe, you let your guard,
But then he shakes—he hits you hard!
One giant whip, a perfect arc,
His drool is flung like modern art.
Your face, your hair, your favorite shirt,
All now soaked—it's extra dirt!
A perfect slap, a sticky fate,
You've lost the war, accept your state.
He stares at you with love so true,
No guilt, no shame, no single clue.
For in his world, through joys and rules,
There's only one—drool rules!

The Floor is Lava, but Worse

You tiptoe round, you dodge the spots,
The floor's a map of wet, dark dots.
A careless step, your socks now soaked,
Another victim—totally cloaked.
You fetch a mop, you start to clean,
But he walks by—a brand-new scene.
The drool drips down, the cycle flows,
A never-ending, slimy prose.
He wags his tail, his head held high,
A joyful look, a happy sigh.
For every mess, he plays the fool,
But deep inside—he knows drool rules!

The Love of a Drooly Dog

Through all the mess, the slime, the spills,
The endless trails, the wobbly thrills—
There's something pure, there's something grand,
In every drop from tongue to hand.
His love is real, his heart so wide,
His slobbery kisses hard to hide.
A little mess? A small price paid,
For all the joy that drool has made.
So wipe your face, accept your fate,
Your life with him is truly great.
For through the years, through fun and fools,
You'll always know—drool rules!

The Game Begins

I wag my tail, I watch you throw,
You shout, "Go get it!" but I say, "No."
The ball rolls far, it hits the ground,
You wait for me—I just lie down.
You point, you plead, you clap, you call,
I blink at you—that's all, that's all.
You huff, you groan, you fetch instead,
I yawn, stretch out, then rest my head.

The Tennis Ball Trap

You bought me balls, you bought me sticks,
But here's the thing—you missed the trick.
You thought I'd chase, you thought I'd run,
But I prefer to watch the fun.
You toss, you cheer, you run and sweat,
While I stay dry and free of fret.
If fetch means work, then let's be clear—
That game's for you, not me, my dear.

The Fetch Imposter

You throw the toy, I run full speed,
Your hopes are high—you think I heed.
I reach the ball, I sniff around,
Then plop right down upon the ground.
You tap your foot, you call my name,
You beg me to return the game.
But here I'll stay, no need to rush,
If you want it back—you fetch, you mush!

The Stick Situation

You toss a stick, it soars so high,
I track it closely with my eye.
It lands, it rolls—I see it there,
I blink once more, then lick the air.
You pace, you wave, you shake your head,
"Go get it, boy!" you yell in dread.
I stretch, I yawn, I scratch my ear,
I think I've made my answer clear.

The Squirrel Exception

You claim I'm lazy—well, that's not fair,
I chase some things, I do still care.
If a squirrel runs, I'll bolt with glee,
So fast you'll barely notice me!
But if it's sticks or tennis balls,
Expect a stare, expect a pause.
One's a chase that fuels my soul,
The other? Eh, not my goal.

The Couch is Better

Why would I fetch when I can nap?
A cozy couch upon my lap.
The world is fine, the ball can stay,
It's right where I last saw it lay.
You keep on trying, I just sigh,
It's clear you're far more eager—why?
If fetching's fun, then let's agree,
You go play and don't ask me!

The One Time I Tried

One time, I fetched—it's true, I swear,
You jumped, you clapped, hands in the air!
But then I learned the cruellest plot—
You threw again? Yeah, I think not.
Why run again? I've learned my lesson,
I'll never start that odd obsession.
I brought it back, now you're on your own,
If you want it—fetch the bone.

The Park Debate

Other dogs chase, they leap, they dive,
They bring things back, they feel alive.
They wag their tails, they race, they run,
But to me? That's not real fun.
I sit, I watch, I sip the breeze,
A life of ease is what I seize.
Why fetch and pant and sweat and drool,
When chilling out is way more cool?

The Ball Collection

There's tennis balls all-round the yard,
Yet still, you try—why work so hard?
If fetch were fun, I'd play all day,
But truth be told? I'd rather stay.
I'll watch you throw, I'll watch you run,
I'll watch you sweat beneath the sun.
It's quite amusing, let's be real—
You fetch for me, so what's the deal?

The Final Answer

So here we are, the game is through,
You've learned by now—this dog won't move.
Throw all you want, just have a blast,
But I'm staying put, I'll always pass.
A life of fetch is not my style,
I'd rather sit and watch you trial.
So here's the truth, let's make it clear:
If you want the ball—fetch it, dear!

The Mysterious Line

I run, I play, I chase with glee,
But there's one spot I dare not see.
A step too close, I freeze in place,
I back away—no need to race.
You call my name, you tap your knee,
Yet something stops the paws on me.
I stare ahead, I sniff, I check,
But cross that spot? Not one more step.
An unseen force, a silent wall—so near, so close, yet feared by all!

The Porch Predicament

The front porch ends, the yard begins,
But I won't go—I won't give in.
I wag, I bark, I stomp and whine,
But step beyond? That's not so fine.
The wind may blow, the leaves may dance,
Yet I won't risk a single chance.
You show me there is nothing there,
But still, my paws won't leave the stair.
To you, it's grass—to me, it's doom, a place where shadows start to loom.

The Imaginary Shock

Once long ago, I felt a zap,
A tiny spark—a little slap.
It told me, "Stop! Don't go too far!"
And now I fear what dangers are.
But here's the thing—the fence is gone!
The zaps have stopped, it's safe—move on!
But I don't trust what I can't see,
This fear's too big, too real for me.
So here I sit, so close—so tense, trapped behind the invisible fence.

The Ball Dilemma

You throw my ball, I watch it soar,
It bounces fast across the floor.
It rolls beyond that dreaded place—
And now we have a real-life case.
I want it bad, I need that ball,
Yet something makes my courage stall.
I whimper, stare, I pace and pout,
But cross that line? I just can't scout.
You fetch instead, you shake your head—some things are better left unread.

The Treat Trap

You lay a treat just past the line,
A juicy snack that should be mine.
You smile, you tease, you urge me on,
But still, my bravery is gone.
A test of will, a choice so tough,
Is it worth it? Not enough.
I stretch, I lean, I reach—then stop,
I back away—my tail's a flop.
Some things you just can't break with snacks, when fear is real, not just some act.

The Other Side

Beyond that space, a world so wide,
With endless smells, and fun to find!
Yet still I stay, I halt and freeze,
As if I'm chained, as if on leash.
The other dogs just dash right through,
They bark, they play, they chase, they zoom.
I watch in awe, I feel so torn,
But fear still whispers, "Stay—be warned."
I know I could, I should, I might—but not today. Perhaps tonight?

The Yard's Edge Mystery

The yard is mine, my kingdom grand,
Yet at the edge—I take my stand.
The wind blows past, it calls my name,
But I don't dare play that new game.
The world beyond is fresh, unknown,
And even though my strength has grown,
I stay inside, my paws hold fast,
For something stops me when I ask.
I don't know why, I wish I knew—but some things aren't for me to do.

The Imaginary Gate

You wave, you walk, you stroll outside,
And call for me to leave my side.
You tap, you clap, you make it clear,
But still, my paws won't wander near.
You step through fine, the path is plain,
Yet something warns me, "Stay—refrain!"
You laugh, you shrug, you try once more,
But I won't move, I know the score.
For though it's gone, I know it's there—this fence exists inside the air.

The Backyard Curse

The yard is safe, the yard is fine,
But take one step? That isn't mine.
I sniff, I glance, I see the path,
But what awaits beyond? I gasp!
Is there a wall, a fence, a trap?
Will something zap me on my back?
I know I could, I should, I might—
But something tells me, "Not tonight."
And so I stay, so near, so tense—forever bound by invisible fence.

One Day, Maybe

One day, I'll step beyond this place,
And run without a hint of brace.
I'll charge through fields, I'll chase the sun,
And never fear the past that's done.
I'll wag, I'll leap, I'll know I'm free,
That nothing holds or captures me.
But until then, I'll wait, I'll sit,
I'll stay behind, just one last bit.

For fences stay—not built, not wired, but deep inside where fear's inspired.

Cats Being Cats

The Witching Hour Begins

The world is still, the night is deep,
The humans sigh, they drift to sleep.
But in the dark, my time has come—
A sudden urge—I must now run!
Across the bed, along the floor,
I ricochet from door to door.
You grumble, groan, and beg for peace,
But zoomies never cease!

The Shadow Stalker

The walls are moving, things aren't right,
I must investigate tonight!
A speck of dust, a ghostly shape,
I pounce! I run! There's no escape!
Under the bed, up on the shelf,
I fight these demons by myself!
You pull the covers, sigh, and hide,
But I must prowl—I must abide.

The Floor is Lava

The carpet's safe, but not the tile,
So I must jump in perfect style!
From couch to chair, from chair to bed,
I land so lightly—on your head.
You grumble, groan, "Not this again!"
But I just leap and run again!
I must escape, I must be fast—
This floor is lava—it won't last!

The Hallway Sprint

I start my race, my paws take flight,
Through halls and doors, I slice the night.
I skid, I leap, I sprint, I soar—
I need to run—just one lap more!
Your groggy voice calls out my name,
"Go to sleep! You've gone insane!"
But I'm too fast, I've got no brakes—
I am the night! The world awakes!

The Invisible Enemy

Did you hear that? Something's there!
A lurking threat—inside the air!
I arch my back, I puff my tail,
I must attack! I cannot fail!
A random shoe, a harmless sock—
I smack it once! I watch it rock!
The battle's won! My war is through—
For now... until round two.

The Bed Sprint Special

Your bed is warm, so safe and tight,
The perfect track for me tonight!
I jump, I dash, I spin, I twirl,
I land—directly on your curls.
You groan, you push, you plead with me,
But this is just necessity!
I've got my zoomies, I must fly,
No sleep for you—but hey, nice try!

The Mystery Meow

I must announce my grand display,
A haunting meow, no more delay!
I yowl, I wail, I sing my song,
At 3 AM—so loud, so long.
You sit up fast, your eyes are wide,
You panic, thinking I have died!
But no, my friend, I'm fine, just grand—
Now pet me with your tired hand.

The Curtain Climb

The moon is high, the stars shine bright,
It's time to climb into the night!
The curtains sway, so soft, so tall—
A perfect place to scale the wall.
I leap, I swing, I dangle high,
I own the room, I own the sky!
But something shifts—I lose my grip—
I crash below... abort the trip!

The Kitchen Raid

The world is still, the house is dark,
But I hear crumbs—a tiny spark!
The counter calls, the sink is near,
What's up there? I must go peer!
A glass? A plate? A silent crime?
I smack it down—oh, perfect time!
You hear the crash, you scream, you swear,
But I'm already outta there!

The Sudden Sprint

I sit. I think. I plan. I wait.
Then—SOMETHING TELLS ME—I CAN'T HESITATE!
I must take off, I must now fly,
I zoom so fast—I don't know why!
You bolt awake, you gasp, confused,
"What's WRONG with you?"—I won't be accused!
For some things can't be questioned, see,
The zoomies simply come to me!

The 4 AM Fade

The chaos ends, my mission's done,
I've conquered night, I've had my fun.
You groan, you toss, you rub your head,
While I curl up beside your bed.
I stretch, I yawn, I softly purr,
The perfect little ball of fur.
So warm, so sweet, so cute—so small...
Until tonight—when I zoom through it all!

The Instant Trap

You sit down once, just for a sec,
A quick little break—what the heck?
Then suddenly, without a sound,
A cat appears—you're locked down.
A tiny weight, so warm, so snug,
You dare not move, you dare not shrug.
Your plans are gone, you're stuck, it's true,
Your lap's no longer owned by you.

The Bathroom Blockade

You really need to take a trip,
But now there's fur upon your hip.
Your legs are numb, your foot is dead,
But there's a cat—right on your head.
You try to shift, you try to slide,
You're met with claws and sleepy pride.
So there you stay, resigned to fate,
Held hostage by your feline mate.

The Work Sabotage

Your laptop's open, work is due,
Your cat walks up—your meeting's through!
A careful plop, a little sigh,
They're here to help—so don't ask why.
Your keyboard's gone, your hands are stuck,
You try to type—well, good luck.
They stretch, they yawn, they knead, they nap,
And now you're fired—thanks a lot, lap!

The Coffee Conundrum

A fresh, hot cup, the perfect sip,
Then suddenly—a little dip.
A tail appears, a paw moves in,
And now there's fur upon your chin.
Your coffee waits, but so does she,
Her sleepy weight won't set you free.
You sigh, you groan, you give up fast—
Your drink is cold, the cat still lasts.

The TV Takeover

You press "play," the show begins,
A peaceful night, no need for sins.
But wait—what's this? A sudden leap!
And now your screen, you cannot see.
A tail blocks half, a paw takes more,
They stretch, they roll, they softly snore.
Your binge-watch dreams are now a wreck,
The cat has claimed your show and neck.

The Phone Intercept

A ringing sound, you grab your cell,
But now you're caught in feline hell.
They sense the call, they sense the chat,
So here they come—your fluffy brat.
A flop, a purr, a head so sweet,
And now your phone is lost beneath.
You try to talk, they start to knead—
The cat comes first—your friend? Indeed.

The Meal-Time Mugging

You sit to eat, you take a bite,
But now your lap is locked up tight.
A gentle weight, a sleepy sigh,
Two eyes peek up, both big and sly.
A little purr, a tiny plea,
You weren't prepared for trickery!
Your fork now stops, you can't resume,
Because your lap is now their room.

The Midnight Capture

You turn in bed, you get all tight,
You're comfy now—well, for the night.
But what is this? A sudden weight?
You must not move—it's far too late!
A cat has perched, right on your chest,
They've found their throne, their perfect nest.
Your arms go numb, your breath is slow,
But moving now? Oh no, no, no.

The Doorway Delay

You grab your keys, you're set to leave,
Then—pounce!—a cat upon your sleeve.
A sudden nap, a firm insist,
Your exit plan does not exist.
You shift, you shake, you try to stand,
They tighten grip—they understand.
The world can wait, your plans can pause,
Because this nap? It's cat law.

The Gaming Glitch

A gaming night, a fun escape,
You're all set up—controller taped.
But then, a flop, a tail, a plop,
Your high-score dreams come to a stop.
The screen is blocked, the buttons pressed,
Your cat has crushed your gaming quest.
And now they purr, so soft, so snug,
Your match is lost—accept the hug.

The Ultimate Betrayal

You stay so still, you hold your breath,
Your legs have lost all sense of depth.
You suffer through, you take the pain,
Because your cat must not complain.
But then, at last, you risk a shift—
They wake! They stretch! They give you grief!
With one sharp glare, they stalk away,
And ten whole minutes later—they're back to stay.

The Silent Stare

I see the glass, I see it stand,
So tall, so proud, so close at hand.
I creep, I pause, I hold my breath,
Then boop!—it falls to its glassy death.
You whip around, you shout my name,
I blink, I yawn—I feel no shame.
It had to go, it had to fall,
And now I rule this empty hall.

The Midnight Heist

The house is dark, the world is still,
Yet I must act—I feel the thrill.
A tiny nudge, a gentle shove,
A plastic cap soars up above.
It spins, it rolls, it hits the floor,
I pause—then push just one thing more.
A distant groan, "Not this again!"
But yes, my friend... yes, yes, it is.

The Vase Was Ugly Anyway

You bought a vase, you loved it much,
A fragile thing, so smooth to touch.
But did you ask me what I thought?
No? Well then... crash!—it meant a lot.
You gasp, you sigh, you hold your head,
Yet I just stretch and beg for bread.
I did you favours, don't be mad,
That vase was ugly—be less sad.

The Pen's Fate

A tiny stick, so long, so thin,
It rests beside where I have been.
I sniff, I tap, it spins around,
Yet still it clings—it won't go down.
A stronger push, a sharper slide,
It teeters once, then leaps to hide!
You fetch it back—I strike once more,
This game will last forevermore.

The Coffee Catastrophe

You set your mug so near to me,
A bold mistake—just wait and see.
The coffee steams, the moment's right,
I raise my paw and flick with might.
The splash, the spill, the utter rage,
You call my name, I feign a gaze.
But truly now, let's tell the truth—
You knew this fate, don't act aloof.

The Butter Incident

A plate of toast, a butter knife,
It sat too long—it had no life.
I saw it there, so dull, so bland,
It needed work—it needed hand.
One push, one plop, one greasy slide,
Now butter's spread both far and wide.
You groan, you weep, you wipe it clean,
Yet I just watch—so proud, serene.

The Plant That Had to Go

Your leafy friend stood tall and bright,
But I knew better—it blocked the light.
I brushed against it, just a test,
A wobble came—it tried its best.
One final push, a graceful fall,
The dirt, the mess—it thrilled my soul.
You scold, you sweep, you fix, you frown,
But trust me—one more's coming down.

The Desk of Doom

Your desk is full, it's stacked so high,
But cluttered space? I can't stand by.
A paper here, a pen right there,
I bat them off without a care.
One by one, they find the ground,
I listen close—oh, what a sound!
The space is clear, I sit up tall,
Until you come... and stack it all.

The One You Tried to Catch

You saw me reach, you saw my aim,
You knew the rules—you know this game.
I nudged, I slid, I took my shot,
You lunged—but no, that glass was caught.
A victory? You think you won?
I wait, I plot—I'm not yet done.
For when you turn, when least aware,
That glass will vanish—then we're square.

The Grand Finale

I've pushed your things both big and small,
From pens to books, I've dropped them all.
Yet still you place them, still they stand,
It's as if you tempt my hand.
You'll never learn, you never do,
This game? It never ends for you.
For every shelf, for every stand,
I live to knock things off by hand.

The Perfect Throne

You sit to work, you start to type,
The coffee's hot, the mood is right.
The screen lights up, you're in the zone,
But here I come—I claim my throne.
I stretch, I flop, I sprawl out wide,
You sigh, you groan—I beam with pride.
The keys beneath feel warm, just right,
This must be where I sleep tonight.
You try to move me? Nice attempt,
But I'm a king—I won't relent.
Your deadline's near? That's cute, my dear,
Now scratch my chin, I'll stay right here.

The Typing Sabotage

You type so fast, the words just flow,
Your hands are moving, minds aglow.
But what's this now? A sudden block?
Your spacebar's jammed beneath my stock.
A tail flicks up, a paw extends,
A single key—your work depends!
But now your screen just fills with junk,
Because I typed—and I'm no punk.
"asldkfhglakjdj!" appears,
I stretch and yawn—what's all these tears?
You shake your head, defeated, sore,
But I just purr, then type some more.

The Heat Seeker

A cat needs warmth, a place to rest,
And laptops truly are the best.
They hum, they glow, they softly purr,
A bed for kings with finest fur.
I spot the screen, I take my cue,
No hesitation—I'm on you.
Your hands protest, I pay no mind,
This spot is mine, it's predefined.
You try again to set me down,
I jump right back—don't make me frown!
For in my rule, there's just one law—
The laptop's mine, accept your flaw.

The Meeting Crasher

Your call begins, you're looking sleek,
You speak with poise—professional peak.
But here I come, all soft and sly,
A tail appears, a paw says hi!
A gasp, a laugh, the screen goes still,
Your boss just saw my regal will.
I stroll across, my tail held high,
For every Zoom call needs this guy.
You move, you push, you beg, you plead,
But I refuse—attention's need!
For what's a call without some flair?
A cat must always make things fair.

The Email Disaster

You type an email, short and neat,
The wording's good, the tone's elite.
But then I strike, I drop my paw,
Your message now is flawed by claw.
"Dear Sir, I hope you"—what was next?
A random "wwww" floods the text!
Your boss responds, "Excuse me, what?"
You shake your head—your cat's a mutt.
I stretch, I blink, I do not care,
For typos are a thing we share.
I fix your work in ways unique,
My edits stand—so do not tweak.

The Game Breaker

You're deep in battle, locked in fight,
Your fingers move—your skills are tight!
A final hit, a winning strike,
But wait! What's this? A fluffy hike?
Upon the keys, my paws descend,
Your screen goes black—this is the end.
You scream, you groan, your game is lost,
And now I sit—a king, at cost.
No victory for you today,
For I've declared a new way.
You game, you type, you try in vain,
But I control this grand domain.

The Assignment Assassin

The essay's due, the pressure's high,
You need to type, the clock ticks by.
But as you write, I take my stand,
A regal loaf upon your hand.
The document? Now blank once more,
Your progress lost upon the floor.
A single paw, a single click,
Deletes your work—my power's thick.
You cry, you weep, you plead, you yell,
But I just purr—this bed is swell.
Next time, remember, when you write—
To save your work before I smite.

The Password Thief

You log back in, you set your code,
A string unique—so well bestowed.
Yet now I pounce, my paws take flight,
The keys go wild—this can't be right.
Your password's gone, a jumbled mess,
Your laptop locks—you're in distress.
I stretch, I yawn, I blink with glee,
The keyboard's warm—it's meant for me.
You call support, your hope runs dry,
They ask, "Did someone type nearby?"
You sigh, admit, with much regret,
"My cat just hacked my whole damn set."

The Social Media Saboteur

A status update? Sounds quite fun,
I press some keys, the job is done.
But wait—what's this? A tweet so odd?
Now friends all think you've lost your bod.
A random post, a garbled phrase,
A message sent in mystic ways.
The internet now knows your name,
But thanks to me, you've changed the game.
You grab your phone, delete it fast,
Yet still, my legacy will last.
For every time you go online,
Your cat ensures the words aren't fine.

The Final Victory

You fight, you try, you push, you move,
Yet I return—I always do.
You set a trap, you block my way,
But kings don't yield—we find a stay.
A cardboard box? A blanket neat?
A cat bed warm? Oh, how so sweet.
But none compare to what you hide—
The keyboard's heat I can't deny.
So give it up, admit defeat,
Your workspace now is obsolete.
I reign, I rule, I own this thing,
For I am Cat, the Keyboard King.

Unusual Pets & Their Quirks

The Legend Begins

I'm small, I'm bright, I swim with flair,
But deep inside, beware—beware!
For though I gleam in orange and gold,
A shark resides within this hold.
I prowl, I lurk, I plot my scheme,
The ruler of this plastic stream.
These tiny pebbles? Mine to own,
This glassy tank? My ocean's throne.
You call me cute? Oh, how you err,
For fearsome beasts, they hide in there.
One day, you'll see, you'll gasp in shock—
A goldfish turned to mighty Jaws!

The Terror of the Tank

I watch, I wait, I bide my time,
This watery world? It's rightfully mine!
The bubbler hums, the filter whirs,
But I decide what now occurs.
You sprinkle flakes—I strike with speed,
A feeding frenzy built on greed!
The other fish all swim with grace,
But I make waves—I own this place!
They cower low, they dart away,
They know the king has come to play.
For though my fins are small, I swear—
A shark-like heart is hidden there.

The Tank Glass Menace

You tap the glass? A bold mistake,
A challenge I am proud to take!
I flare my fins, I bare my might,
Prepare, weak human, for a fight!
I charge the glass, I ram, I glare,
I show no fear—I dare you there!
You laugh, you scoff, but don't forget,
The sea's fierce hunter—not your pet!
One day, this tank won't hold me in,
I'll break right out—I'll grow my fin!
And when I do, beware, beware!
For goldfish sharks lurk everywhere!

The Food Thief

Dinner time—oh yes, it's near!
I sense the food, I sniff the air.
You think I wait? Oh, what a joke,
I hunt it down with mighty strokes!
The others nibble, calm and slow,
But I devour—they fear my flow.
Flakes descend? I snatch, I bite,
A ravenous beast in orange and white.
No meal is safe, no bite is spared,
I take what's mine, I do not share!
For in my heart, I know my place—
The apex hunter of this space.

The Plastic Castle Takeover

This plastic castle, bright and blue,
Belongs to me—not them, not you.
I circle close, I guard the gate,
For trespassers—a fearsome fate.
A guppy swims? I flash my teeth
(Though, well, I lack them—just beneath).
A warning glare, a deadly pose,
One flick of fins, and off he goes!
No fish may stay, no fish may pass,
For I alone rule shark's outpost class.
It's mine, it's law, and make no doubt—
One step too close? I'll chase you out!

The Bubble Blitz

The bubbler gurgles, spews, and swirls,
A water storm of twists and twirls.
The others fear, they dodge, they flee,
But I dive in—it summons me!
I face the stream, I thrash, I fight,
I conquer waves with shark-like might!
The current roars, but I don't sway,
For warriors never drift away.
The tank is vast, yet I remain,
A fearless fish who scoffs at pain.
For though I'm small, let's not pretend—
A shark's true power never ends!

The Daydream of the Deep

One day, I'll swim in seas untamed,
Where whales and dolphins know my name.
No glass to stop me, no plastic walls,
Just endless oceans, mighty calls!
I'll chase the tuna, race the tide,
With sharks and rays right by my side.
My tiny tank? It's just a phase,
For kings like me outgrow their place.
Until that day, I'll wait and plot,
Still knowing I am something hot.
For in this tank, they may not see—
But deep inside, a shark swims free.

The Owner's Misunderstanding

You gaze at me, amused, so smug,
You press your face against this jug.
You call me "cute"? You call me "small"?
Oh, how you do not know at all!
I am no pet—I am a threat!
A fish no predator should bet!
You stare, you tap, you shake your head,
But oceans tremble where I tread.
One day, you'll learn, one day, you'll see,
This tank was never meant for me.
For sharks can't stay in places tight,
And I will break free—just wait for night.

The Flare of Dominance

A new fish comes, so young, so new,
He tries to swim—I block his view.
He flits, he turns, he dodges fast,
But I pursue—he won't surpass.
This is my tank, my world, my rule,
No rookie fish can call me fool.
I chase, I weave, I own the space,
No challenger can match my pace.
So back away, respect my throne,
For I am king, and this is known.
No matter what my size may be,
I rule this tank—so bow to me!

The Final Warning

So listen well, my human pet,
This little fish you think you get?
You feed me flakes, you watch me swim,
But I watch you—your fate is grim.
For one day soon, this tank will crack,
And I will break loose—no looking back!
No bowl will hold me, no fence will stay,
I'll roam the sea and hunt my prey.
So if you laugh, just know, just wait—
A shark's true rise is sealed by fate.
And when that happens, loud and grand—
I'll rule the sea... with iron fins at hand.

The First Slip

I brought him home, so young, so new,
A feathered friend with shades of blue.
I taught him "Hello," I taught him "Bye,"
I taught him words both low and high.
But somewhere in my daily chatter,
He found a phrase that truly mattered.
One slip, one curse, I said too loud—
And now he shouts it at a crowd.
Oh, Polly dear, just say it nice!—
Not "#$%&!!!" once, not twice!

The Dinner Party Disaster

The guests sat down, all dressed so fine,
A fancy meal, some sparkling wine.
The chatter flowed, the mood was bright,
But Polly had his own delight.
"HEY, BIG BUTT!" he screeched with glee,
All heads turned slowly—all on me.
I blushed, I gasped, I shook my head,
"Where did you learn that?" I dread.
Yet Polly squawked with zero shame,
And called my boss the exact same name.

The Grocery Aisle Incident

A peaceful trip, just bread and cheese,
A simple errand—done with ease.
But Polly perched upon my cart,
Prepared to play his cursed part.
A man walked by—Polly took aim,
"TOO MUCH PERFUME!" he loudly claimed.
The lady near just gasped and glared,
I wheeled away, completely scared!
Next time, I'll shop alone, no doubt,
Before this bird gets kicked right out!

The Phone Call Chaos

I took a call, I spoke with grace,
A work discussion—time and place.
Yet Polly, perched, so sly, so bold,
Had other plans that must be told.
"NO PANTS ON!" he yelled with glee,
I died inside—what must they think of me?!
I tried to mute, I tried to hide,
Yet Polly just screamed more with pride.
The call went silent, then came laughter,
My job survived... but barely after.

The Family Gathering Fiasco

Grandma came, she sat so sweet,
A kind old soul, so small, so neat.
I placed some tea, I smiled with charm,
But Polly set off a loud alarm.
"WHERE'S MY BEER?!" he screeched out loud,
Grandma gasped—the room went proud.
"WHO TAUGHT HIM THAT?" she asked, so tight,
I shook my head—not tonight!
But there he sat, with zero shame,
Shouting words that banned my name.

The Vet Visit Horror

A check-up time, a vet so kind,
A simple visit—just stay in line.
Polly perched, so still, so tame,
But then he saw his chance for fame.
"WHAT'S THAT SMELL?!" he squawked so clear,
The waiting room erupted near.
A dog looked guilty, a cat just hissed,
And I became the main culprit missed.
The vet just grinned, my face turned red,
As Polly laughed, inside my head.

The Morning Alarm

Most people wake to peaceful chimes,
Soft, gentle bells or birds that rhyme.
But I wake up to words of fright—
A parrot's roar at morning light.
"WAKE UP, LAZY!" he loudly crows,
I groan, I grumble, I rub my nose.
If I ignore, he escalates,
With "GET UP, STINKY!"—no escape.
A feathered alarm? It's true, it's tough,
But 5 AM? That's quite enough!

The Date Night Debacle

A cozy night, the candles bright,
The mood was set, the date felt right.
We laughed, we ate, we shared a toast—
But Polly had to roast his host.
"OH WOW, BAD HAIR!" he yelled so loud,
My date just blinked, the air turned cloud.
I shushed the bird, I begged for grace,
But he just stared right at my face.
"NOT YOU—THEM!" he squawked, so sly,
Yet somehow... that did not save my guy.

The Holiday Horror

Christmas came, the joy was here,
Presents stacked with hearty cheer.
The family hugged, the room felt bright,
But Polly had his own delight.
"BAD GIFT, BAD GIFT!" he yelled so free,
Right as my uncle stared at me.
The socks were plain, the color meh,
Yet Polly judged with zero stress.
I swear I never taught him that,
Yet now I fear... this bird's a brat.

The Last Straw

I've tried to train, I've tried to teach,
To soften Polly's loose-lipped speech.
But every day, he finds new ways,
To embarrass me in public space.
From "TOO MUCH FOOD!" to "WEIRD MUSTACHE!"
This bird has got no sense of class.
I love him, yes, but I must say,
He tests my patience every day.
Yet when he's sweet and softly coos,
I know, deep down... I always lose.

The Great Houdini

You think I'm small, just fur and paws,
A critter bound by plastic walls.
You lock my cage, secure and tight,
Yet every time—I'm gone by night.
You scratch your head, you search around,
You check the cage—no sign is found.
The wheel still spins, my food's untouched,
But I'm not there—just air and dust.
You wonder how, you gasp in awe,
Yet I just grin—no single flaw.
A twist, a pull, a silent hop—
No lock exists I cannot pop!

The Midnight Escape

The house is dark, the world asleep,
But I prepare—my plan runs deep.
The bars, the latch, the tiny space,
I work with speed, I leave no trace.
One paw, one tooth, one little shove,
I push, I squeeze, I twist above.
The door swings wide, I take my leap,
No cage can hold what must be free!
I dash, I run, I dodge with glee,
Through halls and walls, my victory!
But when the sun begins to glow,
I'm back inside—you'll never know.

The Sock Drawer Hideout

You call my name, you shake my treats,
Yet I remain beneath your sheets.
I scurry fast, I dodge with grace,
A fugitive—this is my place.
The sock drawer's warm, the fit just right,
A nest I build, so soft, so tight.
Your hands dive in, you search in vain,
But I've escaped—once more again.
You lift, you pull, you shuffle through,
Yet I am gone—what will you do?
A little sniff, a twitch, a peek,
From under socks—I'm not that weak.

The Air Vent Adventure

You call my name, but I won't come,
For now, I'm where the wild ones run.
Through tiny holes, past metal bars,
I race beneath the house and stars.
The air vent shakes, the dust is thick,
But I move fast, I slink, I slip.
A breeze flows past, a perfect ride,
Through tunnels deep, I race with pride.
You set a trap, you try to bait,
But freedom calls—I hesitate.
One sniff, one pause, a slight regret—
Yet still, no cage has caught me yet.

The Fridge Expedition

I scurry fast, I scurry low,
To secret spots you'll never know.
Tonight, my mission's food and snacks,
So to the kitchen—no way back!
A climb, a jump, a daring feat,
Upon the fridge, I claim my seat.
The butter? Mine. The cheese? A snack!
No human here will take it back.
Yet then—a sound! Footsteps near!
I freeze in place, I shake with fear.
A blur, a dash, a frantic flight,
Back to the cage—by morning light.

The Tube Escape Plan

You buy me tubes, you build a maze,
You think I'll stay and play for days.
But tubes are paths, not play, my dear,
They lead to freedom, loud and clear!
A twist, a turn, a careful bend,
I find a hole—I see the end!
I squeeze, I push, I pull with might,
And then I'm gone into the night.
You shake the tubes, you call my name,
But I am far beyond your game.
By morning time, I'm back once more,
And you don't know how I left before.

The Couch Caper

You watch TV, you sit so still,
But I am on a midnight thrill.
Behind the couch, beneath the seat,
A hidden path—a hamster's feat!
You hear a scritch, you hear a tap,
You look around—just hear a snap.
You shine a light, you peek below,
But I am stealth, I will not show.
Hours pass, you lose all hope,
You drop your guard—you start to doze.
Then plop!—I'm back, I play it cool,
You never learned my secret rule.

The Bookcase Expedition

You read your books, so proud, so neat,
But I have plots beyond your seat.
A little climb, a tiny sneak,
Upon your shelf, I take my peak!
The tallest book? A stepping stone.
The narrow ledge? My launching zone!
One daring leap, one great escape,
I glide, I land—oh, what fate!
But as I stand, so proud, so tall,
A slip! A fall! A HAMSTER BRAWL!
I tumble down, land in your lap,
And now—you've caught me in the act.

The Under-the-Fridge Trap

I bolt, I dash, I run so sleek,
Through every gap, through every creak.
But what is this? A hidden gate?
A fridge-sized hole—a grand escape!
I dart inside, I hold my breath,
This tunnel leads to furry success.
Yet once I'm in, I start to squirm,
I twist, I turn—I'm stuck! Oh no!
A flashlight beam, a human's sigh,
"Again?" they say—I wonder why?
A gentle tug, I'm free once more,
And back inside... until round four.

The Ultimate Vanishing Act

You double-check, you lock my door,
You reinforce the walls some more.
You say, "Tonight, he will stay in,
No tricks, no jumps, no sneaky win."
Yet when you wake—I'm not inside,
No paw, no tail, no trace in sight.
You scan the room, you search in fear,
But once again... I've disappeared!
Yet where am I? Oh, wouldn't you like to know?
The vents? The couch? The space below?
One day you'll find me, safe and sound,
Until that night, I won't be found.

The Leaf Inspection

You bring me greens, so crisp, so bright,
A feast prepared with pure delight.
You place them down, you step away,
But I must judge before I stay.
I sniff, I nibble, shake my head,
This lettuce feels a bit... half-dead.
A proper meal must meet my test,
And only perfect leaves are best!
You sigh, you groan, you beg, you frown,
But I decide—so take this down!

The Carrot Conundrum

A carrot chunk—oh, what a sight!
But wait—this piece is not quite right.
Too thick, too small, the cut's all wrong,
I'll take my time—it won't take long.
A little taste, a careful chew,
It's not the best? I won't eat two!
You plead, "It's fine!" but I don't break,
A gourmet meal is what's at stake!
For picky pigs like me, you see,
It's carrots first—but only three.

The Cucumber Debate

You place a slice of cucumber fine,
But is it good? The choice is mine.
I take a sniff, I turn away,
Perhaps I'll eat... another day.
Too bitter? Too green? I won't explain,
But this one fails—try once again!
You roll your eyes, you shake your head,
But I choose meals—I must be fed!
Next time, make sure they pass the test,
Or leave the plate! I'll eat the best!

The Bell Pepper Battle

You drop a slice, so red, so sweet,
A crunchy snack—a guinea treat!
But only red, not green or gold,
A fact you should have long been told.
You bring me yellow, what a crime!
It's red or nothing, every time!
You beg, you plead, "Just take a bite!"
I sniff, I snub—this isn't right.
Take back this piece, don't waste my time,
Bring only red—a taste sublime!

The Hay Situation

A guinea pig must munch all day,
And yet you dare bring second-rate hay?!
It's too much dust! It's way too bland!
I shake my head—you must understand!
The strands must crisp, the scent must shine,
This dry old stuff is not divine.
You try again, a better stack,
And now my snack-time's back on track!
The lesson here? It's not so hard,
A critic's taste must be top-chart!

The Lettuce Laws

A plate of greens? Oh, how so nice!
But let's be clear—I have precise
Requirements for leafy snacks,
So let's review—now take this back.
No iceberg, no! It's far too dull,
I demand the greenest pull.
Perhaps some romaine, crisp and tight,
Or butter lettuce—soft, just right.
You get it wrong? I will protest,
A guinea's meal must be the best!

The Fancy Feast

A salad, fine, but here's the thing,
A gourmet pig needs offerings!
Some herbs, perhaps? A bit of dill?
Or basil, mint—oh, what a thrill!
I nibble small, I take my time,
Each leaf should be a work divine!
If one seems off, I drop it fast,
A food so wrong can never last!
The world must know, I set the bar,
For culinary guinea stars!

The Fruit Fiasco

A fruity snack? A nice surprise!
But I must warn—be food-wise!
A strawberry slice? Perhaps a taste,
But make it small, don't go to waste!
Banana? Hmm, I'll take one bite,
But not too ripe, that isn't right.
A grape? A treat? Well, let's be real,
It must be cut, that's the deal.
For fruit must match my high prestige,
A critic's taste? It's fine cuisine!

The Ultimate Rejection

You offer me a mix so bold,
Yet half of this is far too old!
Wilted greens? A shameful sight!
I turn, I squeak—I won't take one bite!
You try again, you pick and sort,
You hope I'll eat—a last resort!
I sniff, I sigh, then take a chance,
A single bite—this may enhance!
It's not the best, but fine—I'll stay,
But only if there's more gourmet.

The Art of Dining

You think I'm picky? That's so wrong!
I simply know what makes me strong!
The finest greens, the freshest treats,
Are all a guinea's right to eat!
You learn my ways, you take good care,
You bring me food that's fit and rare.
No second-rate, no wilted leaves,
No veggies tossed like autumn trees!
So serve me right, and then you'll see,
The picky life was meant for me!

Human-Pet Relationships

The Walk Begins

I grab the leash, you wag with glee,
A simple stroll? We both agree.
But once outside, the roles are blurred,
For you lead first, without a word.
A tug, a pull, I stumble fast,
You dart ahead—I cannot last!
The sidewalk bends, the road is wide,
But I am dragged from side to side!
You sniff, you sprint, you chase, you stray,
While I just fight to stay in play.
So tell me, friend, with leash in tow,
Who walks who? I'd love to know.

The Squirrel Sprint

A peaceful walk, a steady pace,
A leisurely and quiet space.
But then—a flash! A squirrel darts,
And off you go! My world departs!
You yank, you leap, my arm extends,
My balance tilts—this walk descends!
I dig my heels, I pull, I fight,
But you have won—you're out of sight!
Across the grass, you chase, you bound,
While I just flail and hit the ground!
You spin back round, so proud, so true,
As if to say, "Let's go—round two!"

The Sniffing Standstill

You lunge ahead, I race behind,
But then—you stop. A scent to find.
Your nose is down, your tail is high,
The leash goes slack—I just sigh.
A single bush? A mailbox post?
Each one must have the longest toast!
You sniff, you snort, you analyse,
Each smell must be categorized.
I check my watch, I tap my shoe,
But nope, the sniffing isn't through!
A thousand smells, a world to see,
But can we walk? Please, just for me!

The Puddle Panic

A rainy day, a soaked-up street,
Yet still you drag me off my feet!
I sidestep puddles, neat and clean,
But you? You charge right through between!
A muddy splash, a soaking leap,
My legs are wet, my shoes run deep!
You shake, you wag, you laugh, you grin,
While I just sigh—soaked deep within.
A simple stroll? A lovely view?
Not when I'm drenched—all thanks to you!
You tilt your head, as if to say,
"C'mon, let's go! Another way!"

The Leash Tangle Tango

A criss, a cross, a tangled tie,
The leash now loops from low to high.
You twist, you spin, you dodge, you weave,
While I just trip and tug my sleeve!
Around my legs, around my waist,
You double-knot with extra haste!
I try to step, but I can't move,
My balance shifts—I lose my groove!
With one last spin, you sit so proud,
While I just sigh and cry aloud.
You've trapped me well, my walking friend,
And now I'm stuck—until the end!

The Chase is On

A bird takes flight, a cat runs by,
And now you're off—I gasp, I cry!
The leash goes tight, my arms extend,
And suddenly—I'm chasing friends!
You dart through yards, you dash through streets,
I barely keep up on two feet!
A simple walk? That's not your plan,
You sprint as fast as legs can span!
A garbage truck? A barking pup?
Each one must get a close sniff-up!
I'm out of breath, my legs feel weak,
But you're still fresh—so strong, so sleek!

The "Shortcut" That Wasn't

You pick the path, you choose the trail,
But where we go? A muddy tale!
A shortcut claimed, a secret way,
Yet now I'm stuck in grass and clay!
Through bushes thick, through brambles tall,
I duck, I weave, I almost fall!
A simple path? Oh, what a joke!
I'm covered now in twigs and oak.
Yet you don't care, you push ahead,
While I'm just dreaming of my bed.
Next time, I choose where we roam,
And maybe then—we'll make it home.

The "We're Not Done Yet" Standoff

The walk is done, we've made our way,
My arms are tired, my legs dismay.
I turn for home, the door's in sight,
But you have plans—you start a fight.
You plant your paws, you sit real low,
Your tail flicks once—you won't let go.
I pull, I tug, I call your name,
But you refuse—it's still a game!
You dodge, you twist, you pull back strong,
This walk? It must go twice as long!
And so I stand, defeated true—
I ask again, who's walking who?

The Suspicious Car Ride

We're going out? Oh, what a treat!
I wag, I purr, I tap my feet.
A park? A lake? A big surprise?
But then I see your lying eyes.
The road is wrong, the turns are bad,
Your nervous grin—it smells so sad.
And then I see it—big and bold—
That dreaded sign, so cold, so cold.
The vet's dark door, the sterile floor,
A horror place I must endure!
You tricked me once, but now I'm wise,
This trip is filled with pure disguise!

The Waiting Room Woes

A thousand smells, a thousand fears,
The ghosts of cries still haunt my ears.
A nervous dog, a hissing cat,
I must escape!—where is my hat?!
You tell me "shhh," you tell me "calm,"
But don't you see? This place is wrong!
They poke, they prod, they steal my blood!
And you just watch?! I'm done for good!
I plan my break, I scan the room,
A quick escape must happen soon!
But then my name—oh, curse the sound!
My fate is sealed... I'm veterinary-bound.

The Betrayal

You smile and pet, you say, "Relax!"
But here they come, with sharp attacks!
A cold, firm hand upon my back,
A cage of steel—I'm under attack!
They lift, they poke, they check my ears,
A thermometer?! Oh no, my fears!
I kick, I squirm, I fight, I twist,
But these vet fiends do not desist!
How could you, hooman? You stood and watched!
You let them poke—I've been betrayed!
This wasn't love, this wasn't right,
You led me straight into this fight!

The Temperature Trauma

What is that thing? Why is it near?
Keep it away, it's weird and clear!
My tail goes down, my body tight—
Oh, please, dear hooman, save my dignified light!
Too late! Too fast! A horrid crime!
I yowl, I bark, I lose my mind!
You let them do this awful trick,
A cold invasion—way too quick!
The room goes silent, the vet just writes,
While I sit scarred for all my nights.
I'll never trust you ever more,
For this betrayal I must restore!

The Shot That Lied

"Oh, just a pinch!"—you say it soft,
But that was NOT a pinch! Be tossed!
A needle? Sharp?! A STAB, YOU SAY?
Oh, no, no, NO! I won't obey!
I thrash, I twist, I flop around,
I scream so loud—you hear the sound!
The vet just sighs, they hold me still,
I curse them both with all my will!
Then stab! It's done. My rage is real.
You bribed me here for this ordeal!
A simple walk turned dark and grim,
I trusted you! My wrath is dim.

The Scale of Shame

They place me gently on a square,
But what is this?! I do not care!
A number flashes, big and bold,
The vet just hums—I feel so told.
A few pounds more? They start to speak,
They whisper words—I take a peek.
"Too many treats?" they say so low,
EXCUSE ME, SIR—I THINK NO!
The audacity! The shameful weight!
You dare discuss my snack intake?!
I refuse this talk, I turn away,
My perfect fluff is here to stay!

The Ear Inspection Insult

They grab my head, they lift my ear,
Oh, hooman, help! I live in fear!
They poke inside, they shine a light,
I swear this place is pure not right!
I squirm, I twist, I flail, I bite!
I do not need your flashlight sight!
You wouldn't like if I did this,
To your own ears—just think of this!
They poke, they prod, they scribble notes,
I suffer well—I'll hold my votes.
But mark my words, you traitor fake,
I swear revenge when we escape!

The "Good Pet" Scam

"Oh, they were good!"—they smile, they say,
You nod and grin, but I won't stay.
You praise me now, but was it fair?
I suffered deeply—and you're still there!
They scratch my head, they call me "sweet,"
They hand me treats—I sniff in deceit.
What is this game? What is their goal?
I swear they planned to steal my soul!
You take my leash, you lead me out,
I glare, I huff, I drag with doubt.
Oh, hooman dear, you've been untrue,
Just wait—my vengeance waits for you!

The Escape Plan

The moment comes—I'm out the door!
I bolt, I run, I break the floor!
No vet, no needles, not today!
I live to bark another day!
You chase, you beg, you call my name,
But I am free, I leave this shame!
I dash, I sprint, I flee the lot,
You owe me much for what you've wrought!
Next time you try to take me there,
I'll fake my death—I do not care!
For vet visits are purely planned,
A hooman trick! A vile scam!

The Silent Revenge

The car ride home—I sit and glare,
You feel my wrath, you know my stare.
You try to talk, you try to bribe,
But I will not forgive your vibe.
No wag, no purr, no lick, no hug,
Just silent suffering on the rug.
You think I'll break? You think I'll fold?
Oh, hooman, no—I'll make you cold.
I'll wake at 2, I'll cry at 3,
I'll scratch the door for naught but me.
For what you did was cross the line,
And vet revenge… is always mine.

The Sneaky Swipe

You sit to eat, your plate is full,
I watch, I wait—I'm sly, I'm cool.
Your fork lifts up, your eyes look down,
And just like that—I snatch my crown!
A chicken strip, a bite of toast,
A stolen snack I love the most.
You gasp, you chase, but I'm too fast,
This food was mine—it's gone, at last.
You sigh, defeated, shake your head,
While I curl up—completely fed.

The Tabletop Bandit

You tell me "No," you set me low,
But when you turn, I'm up—I go!
I stalk the cheese, the butter knife,
A tabletop adventure life!
A lick, a bite, a little pull,
Your sandwich top is halfway full.
You grab my paws, you scold, you groan,
But I just claim this throne my own.
For if it's left, if you don't see,
Then it's not yours—it's meant for me!

The Napkin Trap

You think I'm done, you think I'm beat,
But crumbs still linger—time to eat!
Your napkin folds, it hides the best,
A little snack still laid to rest.
But oh! My nose, it knows the way,
I nudge, I sniff, it's mine today!
You lift your drink, I snatch real quick,
One sneaky bite—my favorite trick!
You groan, you scold, you plead, you sigh,
But next time—keep it held up high!

The Midnight Raid

The fridge is closed, the house is still,
But hunger calls—I feel the thrill.
I creep, I crawl, I find my way,
A silent thief by night and day.
A nudge, a paw, the door cracks wide,
The treasures cold and rich inside!
A block of cheese? A bite of ham?
Oh, hooman please—you know who I am.
By morning time, the proof is clear—
Your midnight snack just disappeared.

The Pizza Heist

You settle down, the box is warm,
A movie night—your heart's at norm.
The scent drifts out, it calls my name,
And suddenly—we play a game.
You take a bite, I watch, I stare,
You shift the box—I act unfair.
A clever paw, a sneaky dash,
And half your slice is gone in flash!
You sigh, defeated, what a sight!
Well, should've shared, now say goodnight!

The Grocery Bag Gamble

You bring the bags, you drop them down,
You turn your back—I own this town.
A loaf of bread? A juicy pear?
A bag of chips? Let's see what's there!
My paws dig deep, my nose is keen,
Oh, treasures waiting! Smells so clean.
A rip, a tear, a stolen bite,
You rush right in—a panicked sight!
But I am full, my crime is done,
And you learned not to turn and run!

The Dinner Guest Disaster

A fancy meal, a table set,
Your guests arrive—your best one yet!
You light the candles, pour the wine,
But I've got different plans than thine.
A paw sneaks up, a plate tilts low,
A clink, a crash, a loud OH NO!
I lick my lips, the steak was fine,
Yet now your guests just sip their wine.
You shake your head, you glare my way,
But I regret nothing today.

The Sandwich Snatch

A perfect meal, a sandwich stacked,
With layers thick, a lunch well-packed.
You leave it there, just for a sec,
Oh hooman dear, what a wreck.
A hop, a snatch, a chomp—too fast!
Your sandwich life? It didn't last.
You stomp, you chase, but I just grin,
A perfect crime—I always win.
Next time you make a meal so great,
Remember me—and guard your plate.

The Toddler's Weakness

A baby small, so pure, so new,
Yet they have snacks—a dream come true!
A tiny hand, a chubby grip,
One perfect cracker—now it's flipped!
The child just giggles, lets it go,
And I just swoop—a crime so slow.
You watch it happen, shake your head,
Yet I feel proud, completely fed!
Oh little hooman, small and sweet,
Your weakness? Sharing all your treats.

The Final Warning

Oh, hooman dear, now don't you see?
You'll never eat in peace with me.
A fork, a spoon, a snack, a meal,
All fair game—you know the deal.
You push me back, you try, you cry,
Yet I return—I have to try!
For food is meant for all, you see,
And most of all, it's meant for me!
So guard your plate, but not too well,
For I'll be back!—you know it well.

The Morning Routine (As Decided by My Pet)

I wake up slow, stretch out in bed,
But I am late—or so you said.
Your tiny paw taps on my face,
"Now fetch my food—no time to waste!"
I shuffle up, I serve your meal,
You sniff, you glare—this isn't real.
You wanted chicken, not this dry,
You judge me with your piercing eye.
A sigh, a huff, I beg, I plead,
But no, your bowl must match your need.
And so, at dawn, I take my cue,
To cook for you—not me, but you.

The Leash Goes Both Ways

I grab the leash, I call your name,
But you decide we won't play games.
You stare at me, then flop back down,
A heavy sigh—your ears pulled down.
And yet, when you decide it's time,
I must obey—no need to whine.
You scratch the door, you bark, you pace,
Now I must rush—pick up the pace!
Who's walking who? Well, let's be real,
You choose the route, you hold the wheel.
I simply follow, leashed by fate,
My pet commands—I hesitate.

The Bed is Not Mine

I used to own this bed, you see,
Before you claimed it all from me.
A king-size space? Oh, what a joke,
When half the night, I'm halfway broke.
You sprawl, you stretch, you steal my sheets,
I cling to edges, cold defeat.
One little shove—no room for two,
This bed was mine? That isn't true.
By dawn, you yawn, you rise with grace,
While I get up in second place.
I bow, I nod, I scratch your head,
For you own me—I pay the rent.

The Treat Taxation System

I snack in peace, I take a bite,
Yet you appear—a fearsome sight.
Your big, round eyes demand my food,
And I comply—I always do.
One nibble here, one crumb for me,
The rest is gone—I pay your fee.
Your stare is strong, your presence loud,
A ruler's gaze—a throne so proud.
I tell myself I run this home,
Yet here you sit, as if you own.
The truth is clear, I must admit,
I am your servant—this is it.

The Human Summoning Ritual

I hear a thump, I hear a crash,
A mystic sound—a sudden dash!
You call me forth, I must obey,
Your summoning? An urgent play.
A missing toy? A lost desire?
I serve your whims, I don't inquire.
You guide me forth, you point and wait,
I find your sock—you call me great.
Yet when I call, you do not come,
You stare, you blink, you sit, you hum.
It's clear who serves and who commands,
My title's fake—you rule this land.

The Bath is a Betrayal

You roll in mud, you smell like trash,
Yet bath-time brings a wild clash!
You fight, you scratch, you cry, you wail,
As if I sent you straight to jail.
Yet later, fresh, you stroll with pride,
As if I lost, though I supplied.
You flaunt your fur, you flick your tail,
Yet I still wear your bath-time wails.
I say "next week," but we both know,
You'll hide, you'll fight, you'll steal the show.
A bath's betrayal—you declare,
Yet I am wet—you don't seem to care.

The Alarm Clock That Isn't Mine

The sun's not up, the world still sleeps,
Yet you decide it's time for me.
A paw, a chirp, a tiny bite,
I wake to your declared delight.
A tap, a nudge, a loud demand,
You pull my covers with your hand.
No snooze, no rest, just cold command,
Your schedule runs this human land.
Yet when I wake before you do,
You sigh, you stretch, you yawn right through.
You sleep, you snore, with zero guilt,
I see now—this home's been built... for you.

The Door Opens for One

I hear you scratch, you scratch again,
A royal knock, a firm demand.
The door swings wide—your wish is served,
I step aside, my duties learned.
You stroll, you sniff, you pause—you think,
Then turn around, I watch, I blink.
Back inside, back where you came,
And now the game begins again.
I do your bidding, no complaint,
Though you would never do the same.
The door belongs to only you,
I serve, I bow—this much is true.

The Grooming Paradox

I brush your fur, I trim your nails,
You fight, you whine, you thrash and flail.
I work so hard, I try, I sweat,
Yet somehow, I am full of hair.
But when it's you who grooms my head,
You lick, you preen, I'm left for dead.
Your tiny teeth, so sharp, so bold,
A bite! A tug! I must uphold.
You groom, you fix, you set my place,
Yet when I try, it's pure disgrace.
The laws are set, I now can see,
You rule my world—not me, not me.

The Final Truth

I walk, I feed, I serve your needs,
I buy your toys, I fetch your treats.
I carry you, I change your bed,
I follow orders you have set.
You steal my chair, you claim my space,
You judge my meals, you run the place.
I thought I ruled, I thought I led,
But you declared, I serve instead.
So let's be real, the truth is out,
You own this home—there is no doubt.
I was never the owner here,
Just your devoted pet—my dear.

Disclaimer

The poems in this book are purely for fun and entertainment. While inspired by real-life pet antics, any resemblance to actual pets (including yours!) is purely coincidental... or proof that all pets secretly share the same hilarious behaviour!

No animals were harmed, embarrassed, or forced to participate in the making of this book (though a few may have stolen snacks, ignored commands, or stared at me with judgmental eyes).

This book does not provide professional pet training advice—if your dog refuses to fetch, your cat keeps knocking things over, or your parrot has a questionable vocabulary, that's between you and them!

Most importantly, this collection is meant to celebrate the joy, chaos, and laughter that pets bring into our lives. Enjoy, and may your pets continue to be as delightfully unpredictable as ever!

◈ Warning: Reading this book near your pet may result in side-eye stares, tail wags, or demands for extra treats. Proceed with caution!

www.ingramcontent.com/pod-product-compliance
Ingram Content Group UK Ltd.
Pitfield, Milton Keynes, MK11 3LW, UK
UKHW031839210225
455402UK00001B/61